THE TRANSFORMATION DOCTOR

Jordan Storey

The Solopreneur Publishing Company Ltd focuses on the needs of each author client. This book has been published through their 'Solopreneur Self-Publishing (SSP)' brand that enables authors to have complete control over their finished book whilst utilising the expert advice and services usually reserved for traditionally published print, in order to produce an attractive, engaging, quality product. Please note, however, that all final editorial decisions and rights and approval rests with the authors.

Always check with your doctor first before beginning a new exercise regime if you have any health concerns.

ISBN 978-1-8382502-5-6

Printed in the U.K.

CONTENTS

first met Jordan in October 2020, after someone recommended he get in touch with me to help him get the most out of his life and business.

It's interesting when you get someone like Jordan walking into your clinic, someone who is already phenomenally successful and driven and to many people, seem to already have it 'all worked out'.

You might even ask why someone like that would need or want a life coach... well, the answer is simple. Just because someone is already successful, doesn't mean they are content with their situation, doesn't mean they don't still strive to be better, to be more and to achieve more; and in Jordan's case, that translates to helping more people.

What really struck me in that first meeting and still does now when we meet is that Jordan has an unmatched thirst for knowledge and self-development paired with a hunger for success and achievement. This goes part of the way to explaining how he is so effective and productive between sessions, I have honestly never been so impressed as I am by Jordan in the thousands of clients I have worked with in my career.

Obviously, achievement is a subjective concept and is relevant to each of us differently, but as a coach, I strongly believe that our success in life is determined only by our expectation of ourselves. To someone like Jordan, therefore, with unlimited drive, determination, ability and desire, there really is no limit to what he can achieve.

He has already worked with countless professional athletes, celebrities, business owners and thousands of the general public to enhance their lives, and his approach is clear and consistently effective always.

I knew there was 'a book in him' a couple of hours after meeting him and I told him as much, and I guess that is what you are about to read, because guess what, everything he sets his mind to, happens, usually quickly too.

This book is the natural progression for an entrepreneur who is rapidly rising to the very summit of his industry, he already has several successful businesses, apps, seminar programmes, thousands of clients and now this book, and I assure you this is just the start of what is to be a meteoritic rise.

The book contains exactly what society needs right now. At a time where uncertainty and fear open doors to conspiracy theories and quackery in the quest for instant results, this is a breath of fresh air. It is simple, clear, well researched and backed by science, oh, and a few thousand client success stories.

I implore you to read it, to absorb the information it contains and to make positive changes in your life.

I am grateful for my part in Jordan's journey so far and also honoured to be asked to write this foreword. I will finish it off by saying that I am certain the best for Jordan is yet to come, and I for one, am excited to see what it entails.

Jordan, thank you for the inspiration.

Robert Brennan
Life Coach

Jordan's story

never for one moment thought the fact that my mum couldn't cook would turn out to be such a blessing. Her signature dish was 'boil-in-the-bag beef!'. Yes, it was as bad as it sounds. No wonder I was so skinny growing up. But, looking back, in some kind of ironic twist, I think this dish triggered something in me and got me to where I am today. It began my love affair with nutrition and the fitness industry.

Mum and me

Any teasing about how you look can profoundly affect the way you look at life, especially in your early years, and I was no exception. Desperate to conform to the ideal, I tried everything to gain weight and searched out every promise made by the manufacturers, from weight-gaining shakes to all kinds of supplements. Anything I believed might help me in my efforts to become 'buff'! None of which worked.

Worrying about what I looked like came to a head in my last year at high school (for obvious reasons). Well, let's be honest for the opposite sex. By this time, I'd already learned how to cook (out of necessity). I was also starting to gain an interest in how nutrition worked rather than reaching for a quick fix.

Another stroke of luck was living within walking distance to the gym, where I spent many an occasion trying to gain as much knowledge about nutrition and how to build muscle as I could. Looking back, I was pretty relentless in my pursuit

of knowledge, asking all the professionals attending the gym for advice. I found that it helped to accelerate my love of wanting to learn everything I could about fitness and nutrition.

My true passion started to come when I helped other people and saw the positive effects on their appearance and health and the growth in their confidence. So mental health has always been on my radar and even more so nowadays with the greater awareness of its importance.

We are all aware that a poor diet is bad for you, but sometimes the knowledge and motivation isn't always readily available to make those lifestyle differences to your life. I thought long and hard about the name for this book, and for me, it has always been about transformation. I am on a mission to help as many people as I can to make those changes that transform every aspect of their lives.

I understand that trust plays a pivotal role in this process as you want to feel assured that the person you look to for help not only understands how you feel but has the credibility to back up their promises. I am using the word doctor, not in the medical sense of the word, but more informally, in the way a doctor will always try and offer advice and help to make someone feel better.

I have now been in the fitness industry for over 15 years, and I am a fully qualified fitness trainer and nutritionist. However, I am continually looking at ways of

Dad and me

improving my knowledge because I feel academic qualifications are essential. I also know that the knowledge I have gained from listening to many people I have helped transform their lives is as important.

I have helped people of all ages and from all walks of life in their pursuit of health and well-being. A few I have asked to add testimonials for me, just as I feel sometimes it is better to hear about the experiences of others. Some names you may know.

Personally, one of my biggest successes has been helping my father with his long battle with mental health and finding such a positive link between food and behaviour became a pivotal moment for me. To help make such a difference in the life of someone so close to me has meant all the hard work over the last 15 years has been truly worth it.

I also count my successes not just based on passing qualifications (which, of course, are essential) but because of all the fantastic people I have met along the way. Everyone has their own story, but all with one outcome: how they have managed to transform their lives with some of my simple lifestyle changes. Helping people to think more clearly and to have more energy is testimony to how good advice and small changes can bring big rewards.

Opening my first gym and launching a fitness company enabled me to have that personal approach. You learn so much more with instant feedback and understanding what motivates people to change. Helping so many people and seeing not only their bodies transform but also every aspect of their lives has been truly humbling.

I have tried to ensure that in this book, there is something for everyone. The core principles are the same but having created thousands of personal plans over the years, I know that everyone is different. I also know how important it is that you find a plan to suit you and keep you motivated.

It all begins with eating well, so all the recipes in this book have been created to be tasty and simple, with lots of advice on swapping ingredients to suit your tastes.

You do not need to be training to use this book, as I have also made it easy for you to choose recipes for when you are training and when you are not. It is all about making healthy lifestyle choices and putting the passion back into viewing your eating habits as a positive, healthy, and enjoyable experience.

Finally, remember to add love to your food; otherwise, 'dull' food will lead to a 'dull' mind. I am here to take you on that journey and to help you to add in that love.

Jordan Storey

2

Jordan's plan

N/U

by Jordan Storey

The NU Plan

The following plan is designed for each individual to live a healthy life and create their best transformation. The foods I use are carefully chosen to help with this, and the meal timings are very important. The principles are my own unique method which I'm sure you will enjoy. Not only will you reap the rewards of looking great, but you will feel more energized and have a more positive headspace.

As you will see in my meal layout, I have provided you with two versions; one for when you are training and one for when you are on a non-training day.

The training day plan looks like this:

x1 high fat, x1 reduced carb meal x1 high carb PWO meal, and x2 snacks.

The training day plan provides you with a carb-heavy meal post-workout.

After a workout, your glycogen stores need replenishing (glycogen= stored form of glucose, i.e., carbohydrates). Along with a lean protein source will help recover and grow your muscles. So, to cut a long story short, after a good intense training session, your muscles become very taxing on calories, so when you choose one of my high carb PWO meal options, all the calories will be used within the muscles rather than stored as fat. **GENIUS**.

Snacks are in the plan as we all like that little bit of something between meals to help us make it to the next, plus they taste great.

The non-training day plan gives you x2 high fat and protein meals, X1 reduced-carb meals, and x2 snacks.

The high carb meal has gone as you will not be training on this day, so fewer calories are needed. I have chosen higher fats, thus making the body's primary focus to utilize fats as the main energy source rather than carbohydrates. Fat has 9kcal per gram, and carbohydrates only have 4kcal per gram. Meaning you're actually burning more calories by using fat as the primary energy source. **GENIUS**. I know, simple and very effective.

Snacks are in the plan as we all like that little bit of something between meals to help us make it to the next, plus they taste great. So, I hope you enjoy the snack options I have created for you.

The Layout of Your Daily Meals

I would like you to have a reduced-carb meal before bed. I know what you're thinking! CARBS before bed, Jordan, are you mad? I will get fat. Trust me on this one; all will be explained in the next chapter.

The beauty behind this plan is that it is very easy to use and can work round any person's life or work schedule. It doesn't matter what time you train just remember always to have the PWO meal after your session then fit in the rest of the meals throughout the day.

The beauty behind this plan is that it is very easy to use and can work round any person's life or work schedule.

REMEMBER to have the reduced carb meal as your last meal of the day, unless you train on an evening; then, the high carb meal is classed as your last meal.

The non-training day is the same; the reduced-carb meal as your last meal and fit in the rest wherever suits.

Here's the Science!

Let's do a short explanation of some of the basic science on nutrition:

What are calories?
The amount of energy in an item of food or drink is measured in calories.

When we eat and drink more calories than we use up, our bodies store the excess as body fat. If this continues, over time, we may put on weight. However, the same works the other way round; if we consume less and burn more, we will drop weight.

So, you hear everyone talking about macros, and in my book, you will see every recipe will clearly show the macro and calories content in each meal.

But what are they?

MACROS are the three categories of nutrients you eat the most and provide you with most of your energy: protein, carbohydrates, and fats.

So, when you're counting your macros, you're counting the grams of proteins, carbs, or fat that you're consuming.

But why count them? It's the easiest way to track what goes into your body, i.e., how much fat, protein, or carbs you are taking in. Very similar to calories but a little bit more in-depth.

Now let's have a look at each macronutrient and what they do for us.

Understanding what is going on in our bodies is the best antidote to help dissolve many of the myths around 'dieting'.

FAT:
- Promotes absorption of fat-soluble vitamins
- Helps regulate body temperature
- Aids in the production of hormones in the body
- Source of energy
- Protects the organs, nerves, and tissue
- All the body's cell membranes need fat for protection and are needed to grow new healthy cells.

So, society still believes that fat is the enemy, which from the reasons above alone shows how wrong that statement is. But don't get me wrong, there are bad fats, called trans fats, which are found in man-made foods such as chocolate, crisps, etc.

The three types of fats we need to be consuming are:

Saturated fats - animal fats, butter, eggs, cheese, coconut oil.

Monounsaturated fats - nuts, avocado, extra virgin olive oil, peanut oil.

Polyunsaturated fats- flaxseed oil, walnut oil, oily fish.

CARBOHYDRATES:
Why do we need them?

- They are the body's main source of energy
- They are needed for the functioning of your brain,

kidneys, heart muscles, and central nervous system
- Help with your sleep pattern
- They contain fibre which helps with digestion and gut health
- Keeps blood cholesterol levels in check.

So, one of the biggest problems I solve pretty much every day, and the most asked question is, *will I get fat if I eat carbs before bed?* Or, *Jordan, I want to diet; please write me a plan containing zero carbs. I want to get lean for my holiday extra quickly.*

Reviewing the bullet points demonstrate why carbohydrates are so beneficial. Hopefully, this explains why both these questions are just nonsense.

Understanding what is going on in our bodies is the best antidote to help dissolve many of the myths around 'dieting'. Eating carbs late will not make you gain body fat. The human body is incredible. There are no carb police inside saying, 'no carbs after 6pm'. I know I'm joking here, but that's how it can sound. Follow my principles, and I promise you will see the results.

AIDING SLEEP

Also, carbs help with sleep. Now we all love a good night's sleep. Waking up feeling fresh ready to take on that day's challenges has to be a big plus. Carbs are also the body's preferred energy source. So, providing you eat the right carbs will have you fuelled ready to train more intensely, building lean muscle tissue, which means making you leaner—a complete win-win situation.

PROTEIN:
- Growth and maintenance (muscle tissue, bones, and hair)
- Regulates metabolism (metabolism= the process by which your body converts what you consume into energy)
- Production of hormones
- Supports and strengthens your immune system
- Provides energy.

Waking up feeling fresh ready to take on that day's challenges has to be a big plus.

How will I be getting my protein, and from where?

When you look at my recipes, you will see that I mainly use animal-based proteins. They are complete proteins because they contain all the essential amino acids. Amino acids are protein building blocks when you eat a protein source such as chicken, beef, eggs, etc. These proteins are broken down by the body and are formed into amino acids and stored within the body, waiting to be used. However, if you are vegan/vegetarian, you can easily adapt my meals which I will touch on later, using substitutes such as tofu or Quorn as the protein source, but higher amounts will be needed.

> When I have a day off, I love to go out and get in a long walk, as I know later that day, I will be consuming a higher-calorie meal.

Now let's touch on protein powder.

Protein powders are particular favourites with newbies, as there is a belief that these will provide the additional supplements needed when training. However, nothing can substitute receiving your nutrition from eating the right foods.

Reading the food plan in this book, you will notice I have not mentioned protein shakes. I am not saying that there isn't a place for them, however, and I have added some examples of my protein shakes I consume post workout, but just remember eating whole foods are much better for you. You will feel more satisfied, and it will keep you on track, so you are not easily led off the plan to make poor decisions.

I use whey powder after a workout because it's easily accessible, and the body will digest it quickly. It is good for after my workout as the muscles require a quick supply of protein to start muscle recovery and growth. So, please feel free to add in a post-workout shake after your session if it suits your needs. BUT this is not essential to the plan.

A DAY OFF THE PLAN

Whilst following my plan, you will see the flexibility is great, and you still get to taste amazing food, and no day is the same, no eating the old faithful 'chicken and rice' or super shake liquid diets. I have included a treat day one per week, which I believe will be great for your mental state, but also it will not negatively affect your results.

It gives you the freedom to enjoy social events, and future planned events can be worked into your schedule; plus, the day after your off-plan day, you will feel recharged and full of energy, ready for a new fresh week smashing your goals.

Rules to remember on the day off plan:
This doesn't mean that you should go out of your way to

eat every food possible. For example, if you have breakfast planned that day, enjoy it, but then choose a lunch from my plan. Or, maybe have another meal you fancy later for dinner that night, or if you have a meal planned at your favourite restaurant that evening, you may want to follow the plan leading up to that.

By following this approach, your calories are balanced out, and you will not be taking yourself further away from your end goal.

When I have a day off, I love to go out and get in a long walk, as I know later that day, I will be consuming a higher-calorie meal.

Fluid intake:
Aim to drink two to three litres of water per day. You can also consume sugar-free dilute, diet fizzy drinks (no more than one can per day), hot beverages such as coffee, tea, green tea, etc. You can also add sweetener but keep milk to a minimum. A little tip if you struggle to drink water, then add in some fresh fruit. I like to use lemons, cucumber, and fresh mint leaves.

Exercise:
Later in the book, you will see the HIIT sessions I have planned for you. The beauty of this training style is that it only takes 30 minutes out of your day and can be done at your home. You will see significant benefits as it raises your heart rate up and really torches your body fat. You can adjust these workouts to make them easier if needs be.

Why not start with 10 minutes per day and build up?

You can do one workout per day or less, depending on your life schedule. Remember, recovery is also essential, so do not overdo it. I would recommend four workouts per week.

You can also use your current workout schedule if that works for you. However, the diet alone will get you great results. You do not need to attend a gym, or if you have injuries stopping you from exercising, do not worry.

Going out on walks is also a great form of exercise, plus the benefits it gives you, and your mental well-being is great. Remember, the more you exercise, the more energy you will have, meaning you will live a fuller life and be able to take on day-to-day challenges.

What is **NU**?

NU by Jordan Storey' launched in August 2021.

From having huge personal success prior and seeing hundreds of clients each month, I created a new company with an app that will give a one-to-one experience on a much bigger scale; no matter where you live in the world, you can take part. NU is designed to provide you with the complete transformation from the body to the mind. So, this is for you, whether you want fat loss, weight gain, improved health, improved fitness levels, more energy, lifestyle changes, or even just to be part of our community.

DULL FOOD = DULL MIND

I have studied mental health, and I have seen first-hand the impact poor mental health can have on someone's life. It's clear to see the foods we eat play a significant role in our mental well-being. If you watch my short video clips on Instagram of my cooking, you will notice I often use the phrase 'Adding love into your meals'.

Meaning don't cook the same old boring foods that don't look very appetizing. Not only do they taste bad, but they will also give your brain an adverse effect before eating them. Instead, cook with plenty of love, add in plenty of colourful vegetables, fruits and make it more exciting with fresh herbs and sauces. Then, when you sit down to eat a lovely-looking meal, your brain will have a much more positive effect, and you will feel great.

> Instead, cook with plenty of love, add in plenty of colourful vegetables, fruits and make it more exciting with fresh herbs and sauces.

WHAT IS NU TO YOU?

By reading this book, you will learn about nutrition and exercise, which you can put into everyday life. As a result, you will live a healthier and more energized life and a positive mindset. You will also look and feel great.

Your sleeping patterns will also be improved with my techniques and approach to dieting.

You will become the NU YOU.

WHY WILL I SEE IMPROVED SLEEP?

Ok, so you may have noticed that using my plan, you will always have a carb meal before bed!

The main reason is that carbohydrates trigger insulin which then increases the amount of tryptophan and serotonin. These two brain chemicals cause drowsiness and reduced alertness; that's why after a large meal, you generally feel sleepy. But also, with improved sleep, you will improve the hormone called Leptin, which is responsible for communicating with the brain that you have enough stored fat, which curbs your appetite and signals the body to burn calories normally and prevents excessive eating.

Let's Get Started

You can't climb a mountain with pebbles in your shoes.

Time to let go of everything holding you back, goals need hitting and any distractions will get in the way.

Let's start by creating the perfect environment for a healthy lifestyle. Clear the cupboards of any bad foods, chocolate, sweets, crisps, etc. That way, they will not enter your mind and take away the possibility of grabbing that little snack whilst your dinner is cooking for a quick sugar fix. Enjoy the naughty treats in moderation, then when you go out to socialise you can eat things guilt-free, which is the much healthier approach. You should not feel guilty every time you go out and enjoy something off-plan. Once you have set the perfect environment, you can start taking steps towards the NU you; having a much clearer path will make it easier.

Set goals

Goals are important in the sense that they give you direction in life. No matter how big or small the goal is.

Having goals is like having a map. You know where you are heading, and this gives you zest, motivation, more energy, and a reason to get up in the morning.

A favourite quote of mine from Tony Robbins:

Enjoy the naughty treats in moderation, then when you go out to socialise you can eat things guilt-free, which is the much healthier approach.

"Setting goals is the first step in turning the invisible into the visible."

You will achieve more when you reach your goal. It gives you a taste of victory; with this, you will want that feeling and taste again. It becomes almost addictive.

They help keep motivation. It's easy to put off tasks until tomorrow when there is no goal on the line.

For example, let's consider the life of an athlete. If they have to get in shape for, say, the Football or NFL season, believe they are going to be working out each and every day, whether they feel-good or not, whether they are sore or not, whether they are tired or not, whether they want to or not because they have a goal.

They have a destination.
Their desire to achieve their goal keeps them in the gym when they would much rather skip.

In much the same way, having a goal will keep you motivated!

Create good habits

Study shows that it takes eight weeks to create a new habit.

Once you have set the perfect environment, you can start taking steps towards the NU you; having a much clearer path will make it easier.

Keep this in mind and repeat the daily activities to stay on track. Go back to the goals you have set yourself, keep them on sight, on the fridge door maybe. Write down small wins you do each day, whether attending a gym class, going for a walk, taking up a new hobby, cooking a new meal, or completing a full day on the plan. Finally, write down your gratitude and look back at that regularly to see how far you have come.

Food prep

We have all heard the saying 'fail to prepare or prepare to fail'.

Some great reasons here on why preparation is key:

· Improves your time management
· Helps you stay on track
· More cost-effective
· Helps you regulate portion control
· Creates a new habit

Also, just a little tip from me: DO NOT GO SHOPPING WHEN HUNGRY!

I am sure we have ALL done this – I know I have, and I've added all sorts to my trolley, crisps, donuts, fizzy drinks, candy, the lot.

Food Essentials

Check out the essentials. I always make sure I have these in. Making it much easier to stay on track and not be tempted to order in some fast food when stocks are low:

- Oats
- Rice
- Potatoes
- Seasonings and Spices: salt and pepper, garlic, chilli, paprika, cinnamon, Cajun, and Peri Peri
- Olive oil
- Coconut oil
- Eggs
- Yogurt
- Frozen veggies
- Tinned tuna
- Lentils

The fact you write down the meals you have chosen instantly makes you want to stay on track.

Food diary and workout planner

A food diary can be a useful tool in this process. It can help you understand your eating habits and patterns and help you identify the foods. Also, if you track how you feel on a certain day, you can look back and see your mood patterns; there may be a link between both food and mood. It is also great for accountability. The fact you write down the meals you have chosen instantly makes you want to stay on track.

A workout planner is a great tool to have. If you forward plan your training sessions, it will excite you to complete them and challenge yourself.

If you are following my workouts, make sure you track your progress in your planner, this way, you can look back and see how much you have progressed.

5

High fat and protein meals

Fried Eggs with Ham

Ingredients:
2 Eggs
100g Ham (Canadian Bacon)
Handful of Mushrooms
Handful of Cherry Tomatoes
Handful of Spinach

Method:
- Preheat a frying pan on medium heat, use cooking spray or coconut oil
- Cook ham for 2 minutes on each side, or you can use the pre-cooked oven-baked ham. If using the pre-cooked ham, heat in the frying pan
- Add sliced mushrooms, tomatoes, and spinach to the pan and sauté for 5 minutes
- Once cooked, plate
- Crack both eggs in the frying pan and cook until your desired style is achieved
- Serve with seasoning of your choice
- Enjoy!

Nutritional Value:
Calories: 250
Carbs: 1g
Protein: 32g
Fats: 13g

Smoked Salmon with Avocado and Feta Cheese

Ingredients:
80g Salmon
½ Avocado
Handful of spinach
Handful of tomatoes
25g Feta
25g Walnuts
1 Tbsp Oil

Method:
- Mix the feta cheese, chopped walnuts, and olive oil into a bowl
- Slice the avocado and tomatoes
- Arrange the spinach, avocado and smoked salmon on a plate
- Serve with sliced tomatoes and feta mix on top
- Pepper to taste
- Enjoy!

Nutritional Value:
Calories: 610
Carbs: 7g
Protein: 26g
Fats: 52g

Greek Yogurt with Mixed Nuts and Berries

Ingredients:
150g Greek Yogurt
30g Mixed Nuts
80g Berries

Method:
- Weigh out all the ingredients
- Add the Greek yogurt to a bowl
- Top with nuts and berries
- Enjoy!

Nutritional Value:
Calories: 200
Carbs: 13g
Protein: 14g
Fats: 10g

Jordan's Protein-Packed Shake

Ingredients:
1 Scoop Protein Powder
2 Tbsp Greek Yogurt
50g Mixed Berries
½ Avocado
1 Tbsp of Honey (One squirt from bottle)
250ml of Almond Milk

Method:
- Weigh out all the ingredients
- Add to blender with the almond milk and honey
- Add ice
- Enjoy!

Nutritional Value:
Calories: 354
Carbs: 20g
Protein: 28g
Fats: 18g

Jordan's Peanut Butter Smoothie

Ingredients:
1 Scoop Protein Powder
1 Tbsp Peanut Butter
50g Blueberries
Sprinkle of Cinnamon
Handful of Spinach
Tsp of Chia Seeds
250ml Almond Milk

Method:
- Weigh out all the ingredients
- Add to blender with almond milk
- Blend with ice
- Serve with a teaspoon of chia seeds on top
- Enjoy!

Nutritional Value:
Calories: 340
Carbs: 20g
Protein: 29g
Fats: 16g

Feel-Good Shake

Ingredients:
1 Scoop Protein Powder
¼ Cucumber
5 Medium Mint Leaves (add more for stronger mint flavour)
Handful of Spinach
30g Cashew Nuts
250ml Coconut Water

Method:
- Weigh out all the ingredients
- Add to blender with coconut water and ice
- Once blended your shake is ready to be served
- Enjoy!

Nutritional Value:
Calories: 310
Carbs: 17g
Protein: 27g
Fats: 14g

Cheesy Scrambled Eggs with Chorizo

Ingredients:
3 Eggs
50g Chorizo
40g Shredded Mozzarella or Feta

Method:
- Spray a frying pan with cooking spray and place on a medium heat
- Add the sliced chorizo and cook for 5 minutes
- Crack the eggs into a bowl, whisk together, add the grated cheese and season with salt and pepper
- Add the cooked chorizo to the bowl and mix together
- Add the mixture to a deep pan with cooking spray to cook and mix for 2-3 minutes or until desired texture is reached
- Once cooked, serve with chilli flakes or sauce of your choice
- Enjoy!

Nutritional Value:
Calories: 562
Carbs: 3g
Protein: 36g
Fats: 43g

Mozzarella or Feta Cheese Omelette

Ingredients:
3 Eggs
25g Mozzarella or feta
Handful of spinach
Handful of mushrooms
½ Handful of cherry tomatoes

Method:
- Weigh ingredients and slice your mushrooms and tomatoes
- In a mixing jug add your eggs, spinach, sliced mushrooms, and tomatoes and whisk together adding salt and pepper
- Add cooking spray to a frying pan and put on a medium heat
- Now that your frying pan is heated add the mixture
- Once the mixture begins to cook and firm up but still runny add the preferred cheese on top
- Using a spatula, ease around the edges of the omelette and fold it in half
- After 1 minute flip the omelette on to the other side and cook for a further minute and until golden brown
- Once cooked slide the omelette onto a plate and serve with a side of spinach and sliced tomatoes and preferred sauce
- Enjoy!

Nutritional Value:
Calories: 290
Carbs: 5g
Protein: 23g
Fats: 19g

Steak with Asparagus and Poached Egg

Ingredients:
200g Steak
1 Egg
Asparagus

Method:
- Preheat the oven to 200c
- Spray cooking spray over the asparagus and season with desired spice blend, add to the oven and cook for 15 minutes.
- Boil a pan of water on high heat
- After 5 minutes of the asparagus going in the oven, place a frying pan on high heat on the stove
- Heat 1 teaspoon of coconut oil, coating the pan. Season your steak with salt and pepper
- Add the steak to the frying pan and cook on both sides for 5 minutes for a medium rare steak, cook longer for a more well-done steak
- Once you remove the steak from the heat, crack the egg in the boiling water and let it poach for 2 minutes
- Let the steak rest
- Take the asparagus out of the oven and plate
- Enjoy!

Nutritional Value:
Calories: 400
Carbs: 1g
Protein: 50g
Fats: 21g

Steak and Mozzarella Salad

Ingredients:
200g Steak
Salad
30g Mozzarella

Method:
- Add 1 teaspoon of coconut oil to a frying pan and put on a high heat
- Pan fry the steak on each side for 5 minutes, cook longer for a more well-done steak
- In a large bowl mix together preferred salad ingredients such as -lettuce/spinach, cucumber, tomatoes, peppers, onion, olives
- Once your salad is complete add sliced mozzarella
- Add sliced cooked steak on top of the mozzarella salad
- Serve with a low-calorie salad dressing or glazed balsamic vinegar
- Enjoy!

Nutritional Value:
Calories: 490
Carbs: 6g
Protein: 51g
Fats: 35g

Chicken and Mango Salad

Ingredients:
200g Chicken
100g Mango
½ Orange
Handful of tomatoes
Handful of lettuce and spinach
½ Handful of chopped olives
1 Tbsp of olive oil

Method:
· Combine and mix all the salad ingredients into a large bowl (mango chunks, tomatoes, olives, lettuce, spinach, olive oil)
· Preheat the oven on 180c and season the chicken with your desired spice mix
· Once seasoned, add the chicken to a baking tray with tin foil and add to the oven to cook
· Cook the chicken for 30 minutes, turning it over halfway
· Now the chicken is cooked, remove from the oven and slice into smaller pieces
· Once sliced add to the mango salad
· Squeeze a fresh orange on top and serve
· Enjoy!

Nutritional Value:
Calories: 422
Carbs: 16g
Protein: 43g
Fats: 19g

Chicken Chorizo and Feta with Spinach

Ingredients:
200g Chicken
50g Chorizo
25g Feta
Handful of spinach

Method:
- Season your chicken with your preferred spice, pepper and salt, once seasoned dice your chicken
- Slice your chorizo
- Preheat a frying pan with cooking spray and add your diced chicken
- After 5 minutes of cooking the chicken add your sliced chorizo
- Cook both for a further 3 minutes and then add the spinach
- Continue cooking the ingredients for a further 2 minutes and until the chicken is golden
- Once cooked you can serve onto a deep dish adding your feta cheese on top
- Enjoy!

Nutritional Value:
Calories: 500
Carbs: 1g
Protein: 62g
Fats: 28g

Chicken with Garlic Mushrooms and Vegetables

Ingredients:
200g Chicken
150g Mixed mushrooms
100g Butternut squash
½ Courgette/zucchini
1 Garlic clove crushed
Salt
Pepper

Method:
- Slice up the mushrooms, garlic, zucchini, and squash.
- Add mushrooms and garlic to a frying pan with 1 teaspoon of coconut oil on medium heat.
- Dice the chicken and season with your choice of spice
- Once seasoned, add to the mushrooms and garlic that are already cooking
- After 5 minutes add the zucchini and squash
- Sauté for 10 minutes
- Serve adding salt and pepper to taste
- Enjoy!

Nutritional Value:
Calories: 310
Carbs: 20g
Protein: 42g
Fats: 2g

Lamb Shank with Jordan's Homemade Tzatziki and Vegetables

Ingredients:
Lamb shank
Mediterranean veg
1 tbsp olive oil
Thyme
Rosemary
1 Garlic clove crushed
Sprinkle of Smoked paprika
Salt
Pepper
Cucumber
Mint
Greek yogurt

Method:
- Preheat the oven to 180c
- Season the lamb with olive oil, salt, pepper, thyme, and garlic
- Place on a baking tray with tin foil and add to the oven and cook for 40 minutes
- Slice your Mediterranean vegetables and add to a baking tray with tin foil
- Spray cooking spray on top of the vegetables and add salt, pepper and smoked paprika
- After 10 minutes of the lamb cooking add the vegetables to the oven and cook for 30 minutes

Method for the Tzatziki:
- Add the yoghurt to a small bowl
- Grate into the bowl the green part of the cucumber and squeeze out the liquid adding a pinch of salt
- Add the garlic and mint and mix all together
- Once the vegetables are cooked serve on a plate adding the cooked lamb on top and garnish with fresh rosemary thyme
- Serve on the side the homemade tzatziki
- Enjoy!

Nutritional Value:
Calories: 640
Carbs: 18g
Protein: 48g
Fats: 47g

Watermelon, Mint and Feta Salad

Ingredients:
30g Feta
100g Watermelon
25g Pecans
Mint leaves
Spinach
Balsamic vinegar

Method:
- Dice the watermelon and feta cheese
- Chop the mint leaves finely
- Add the spinach to a deep dish, large bowl, or plate
- Add in the finely chopped mint leave and mix together with the spinach
- Add the diced watermelon and feta cheese
- Sprinkle the pecan nuts on top
- Serve with a glazed balsamic vinegar dressing
- Enjoy!

Nutritional Value:
Calories: 278
Carbs: 11g
Protein: 9g
Fats: 25g

Almond Crusted Cod with Courgetti

Ingredients:
200g Cod
40g Flaked crushed almonds
200g Courgette
2 Egg whites
Salt
Pepper

Method:
- Add 2 egg whites to a bowl, adding salt and pepper and dip your cod into the egg white mixture
- Once dipped cover one side in almond flakes
- Preheat oven to 180c and add the cod to a baking tray with tin foil and cook for 20 minutes
- Season and boil vegetables of your choice for 10 minutes
- If not already spiralised using your machine spiralise a courgette
- Season with salt and pepper and boil in a pan 5 minutes
- Serve on a plate once the cod and courgette are cooked with seasonal vegetables of your choice
- Enjoy!

Nutritional Value:
Calories: 460
Carbs: 8g
Protein: 50g
Fats: 23g

Jordan's Sticky Pork

Ingredients:
2x Belly pork slices
Stir fried vegetables
1 Tsp coconut oil
Salt
Pepper
Chilli flakes

For the sauce:
2 Tbsp soy sauce
1 Tbsp maple syrup
1 Tsp rice wine vinegar
1 Tsp corn flour
Chilli

Method:
- Slice the belly pork into small pieces and season with salt, pepper, and chilli flakes
- Add coconut oil to a frying pan and add to a medium heat and cook the sliced belly pork for 10 minutes
- Add in prepared stir fry vegetables of your choice and add garlic and cook for a further 5 to 10 minutes

Method for Sticky Homemade Sauce:
- Mix together all the ingredients for the homemade sticky sauce in a small bowl
- Once all cooked and prepared serve your pork stir fry along with the homemade sticky sauce
- Enjoy!

Nutritional Value:
Calories: 400
Carbs: 15g
Protein :18g
Fats: 25g

Sauce: 100cals

Beef and Avocado Chilli

Ingredients:
200g Minced beef
Mixed peppers
¼ Tin of tomatoes
50g Kidney beans
1 Tsp chilli powder
1 Avocado
1 Onion
1 Garlic clove crushed
½ Chilli sliced and seeded
200ml Beef stock

Method:
- Add cooking spray to a frying pan on medium heat
- Cook sliced onions, garlic, and chilli for 2 minutes
- Now add mixed cut peppers and cook for a further 3 minutes
- Add the spices and herbs
- Add the beef mince and cook until browned
- Once the mince has browned add more seasoning if needed and the tinned tomatoes, plus the beef stock with 200ml of water
- Please allow the chilli to simmer for 20 minutes, adding the kidney beans after 10 minutes
- Prepare, season and boil for 10 minutes your chosen vegetables
- Once cooked you can serve the chilli in a deep bowl with your vegetables on the side and the sliced avocado on top
- Enjoy!

Nutritional Value:
Calories: 510
Carbs: 28g
Protein: 44g
Fats: 29g

Grilled Salmon with Root Mash and Greens

Ingredients:
1 Salmon fillet
100g Sweet potato
50g Carrots
50g Swede/rutabaga
Green veggies
Salt
Pepper

Method:
- Boil a medium pan of water
- Preheat the oven to 200c
- Peel and dice the sweet potato, carrots, and rutabaga, once the water is boiling, add them to the pan to boil for 10 minutes
- Season the salmon to your liking and place under the grill for 10 mins each side
- Prepare, season, and boil your green vegetables for 10 minutes
- Drain your vegetables and using a potato masher or electric mixer, mash them all together, season with salt and pepper
- Once all cooked serve on a plate with a lemon wedge
- Enjoy!

Nutritional Value:
Calories: 424
Carbs: 31g
Protein: 40g
fats: 15g

6
Reduced-Carb Meals

Wakeup Call Shake

Ingredients:
1 Scoop protein powder
30g Oats
1 Shot of espresso coffee
250ml Oat or coconut milk

Method:
- Weigh out all the ingredients
- Add to the blender with 250ml of milk of choice and ice
- Add in the shot of coffee
- Blend and enjoy!

Nutritional Value:
Calories: 337
Carbs: 37g
Protein: 28g
Fats: 8g

Mango Blast

Ingredients:
1 Scoop protein powder
50g Mango
50g Pineapple
Handful of spinach
Sprinkle of cinnamon
1 Tsp of honey
250ml Unsweetened almond milk

Method:
- Weigh out the ingredients and add to the blender
- Add 250ml of unsweetened almond milk or coconut water plus ice
- Blend and enjoy!

Nutritional Value:
Calories: 223
Carbs: 24g
Protein: 23g
Fats: 4g

Banana Porridge Bowl

Ingredients:
30g Oats
1 Scoop of protein powder
1 Banana
25g Pecans
1 Tsp Maple syrup
200ml Oat milk

Method:
- Mix the porridge oats with the oat milk in a large microwavable bowl
- Microwave until cooked
- Leave to stand for 1 minute
- Mix the protein powder into the cooked porridge oats
- Top with sliced banana, pecans, and a drizzle of syrup
- Enjoy!

Nutritional Value:
Calories: 500
Carbs: 69g
Protein: 31g
Fats: 12g

Porridge Berry Bowl

Ingredients:
40g Oats
50g Strawberries
50g Blueberries
1 Tbsp Almond butter
Sprinkle of coconut shavings
250ml Unsweetened coconut milk

Method:
- Mix the porridge oats with the coconut milk in a large microwavable bowl
- Microwave until cooked
- Leave to stand for 1 minute
- Top with sliced strawberries, blueberries and a tablespoon of almond butter
- Serve topped with coconut shavings
- Enjoy!

Nutritional Value:
Calories: 340
Carbs: 41g
Protein: 9g
Fats: 16g

Fancy French Toast with Bacon

Ingredients:
1 Slice thick-cut whole grain bread
2 Large eggs
2 Slices bacon
200ml Unsweetened almond milk
100ml Fresh orange juice
1 Tsp Vanilla extract
Sprinkle of cinnamon
Sprinkle of nutmeg
1 Tbsp of maple syrup

Method:
- In a large bowl, whisk together the eggs, almond milk, orange juice, vanilla, cinnamon, nutmeg, and maple syrup
- Place the mixture into a shallow dish and add the bread slice into the mixture and allow to soak for 2 minutes each side
- Add bacon slices into a heated pan using Cooking spray until cooked
- In another heated pan, using cooking spray cook the bread on each side for 3-4 minutes
- Serve the French toast and add the bacon and syrup topping with blueberries
- Enjoy

Nutritional Value:
Calories: 386
Carbs: 44g
Protein: 18g
Fats: 16g

TOP TIP

Remove the egg
to make this recipe
Vegan

Chilli Avocado and Egg on Sourdough Toast

Ingredients:
1 Slice of sourdough bread
2 Large eggs
½ Avocado
Feta cheese (optional)
Chilli flakes
Lemon

Method:
- Prep the avocado by cutting in half and spoon one half of the avocado into a small bowl
- Add a squirt of lemon juice and sprinkle a small amount of chilli flakes into the bowl, and mash together with a fork
- If not already prepared, then pre-cut a slice of sourdough bread
- Bring a deep pan of water to boil adding a pinch of salt
- Crack the egg into the water and leave to cook for 3-4 minutes
- Toast the sourdough bread whilst the eggs are cooking
- Once toasted spread the avocado over the sourdough bread
- Remove the eggs from the pan using a slotted spoon and place carefully on top of the avocado sourdough toast
- For cheese fans, finish with a topping of feta cheese
- Enjoy!

Nutritional Value:
Calories: 360
Carbs: 26g
Protein: 17g
Fats: 22g

Overnight Oats with Cinnamon

Ingredients:
30g Oats
100ml Oat milk
2 Tbsp Greek yogurt
1 Tsp Chia seeds
Sprinkle of cinnamon
Toppings of choice

Method:
- Add the rolled oats to an airtight container and pour over with oat milk
- Layer with Greek yoghurt, chia seeds, add a sprinkle of cinnamon and shake to mix the ingredients
- Refrigerate overnight
- Add toppings of your choice, i.e., fruit, peanut butter, maple syrup, honey, etc
- Enjoy!

Nutritional Value:
Calories: 246
Carbs: 29g
Protein: 9g
Fats: 10g

Jordan's American Breakfast

Ingredients:
2 x Bacon slices
2 x Chicken sausages
2 x Eggs
150g White potato
1 Beef tomato
½ Onion
Handful of mushrooms
American mustard
25g Fresh mozzarella
Garlic
Sat
Pepper

Method:
- Heat the oven to 200c and preheat your baking tray
- Peel and cut the potatoes into small chunks roughly the same size as each other
- Place them on to the hot baking tray and roast for 45 minutes or until golden and crispy (make sure you turn the potatoes over once or twice whilst they are cooking)
- Slice the bacon, sausages, mushrooms, onion, and tomato
- Once the potatoes are cooked, heat a large pan with cooking spray and place the chopped bacon and sausages to cook adding garlic, salt, and pepper
- After 2 minutes, add the sliced mushrooms, onion, and tomato to cook
- Once all cooked, add the roasted potatoes to the heated pan
- Crack the eggs into the pan and mash them all together
- Top with mozzarella and American mustard and leave to cook for 1 minute
- Serve with hot sauce
- Enjoy!

Nutritional Value:
Calories: 580
Carbs: 34g
Protein: 30g
Fats: 27g

Jordan's Buckwheat and Blueberry Jam Pancakes

Ingredients:
40g Buckwheat flour
1 Tsp Baking powder
1 Egg
100ml almond or oat milk
50g blueberries
Agave or maple syrup

Method:
- Whisk the eggs and milk together in a jug
- Sieve the flour into a mixing bowl and add the baking powder
- Gradually add the wet ingredients to the dry and whisk, adding a pinch of salt
- Using cooking spray, heat a frying pan on medium heat and add a large teaspoon of the batter mix to the pan to make a pancake
- Once golden, flip the pancake over and repeat with the remainder of the batter
- Add the blueberries to a deep pan with 100ml of hot water for 5 minutes and mash with a fork to create the jam
- Serve the pancakes and top with the blueberry jam and finish with a drizzle of agave/maple syrup
- Enjoy!

Nutritional Value:
Calories: 328
Carbs: 42g
Protein: 13g
Fats: 6g

Jordan's Chocolate Orange Yogurt Bowl

Ingredients:
170g 0% Greek yogurt
1 Orange
2 Squares dark chocolate
30g Pecans

Method:
- Add the yoghurt to a deep bowl
- Add pecans and half of the dark chocolate chopped to the yoghurt
- Slice the orange in half, cut one half into small pieces and add to yoghurt and squeeze the other half over
- Finish topped with melted dark chocolate
- Enjoy!

Nutritional Value:
Calories: 255
Carbs: 27g
Protein: 19g
Fats: 8g

Cheeky Chicken and Pineapple Pitta

Ingredients:
150g Chicken
1 x Pitta bread
1 Handful of spinach shredded
1 Handful of cherry tomatoes chopped
½ Handful of olives chopped
½ Handful of shredded carrot
1 Lemon (to squeeze over the salad)
100g Pineapple
25g Mozzarella
Hot sauce

Method:
- Using a griddle pan, spray with cooking spray and cook chicken breast (7-10 minutes each side) until cooked, adding seasoning of your choice.
- Prep the salad in a large bowl whilst the chicken is cooking, once prepared add the salad, including pineapple pieces to your pitta/s
- Once the chicken is cooked, slice the breast into strips and allow to cool for 1 minute
- Add sliced chicken inside your pitta/s
- Serve with grated mozzarella and hot sauce
- Enjoy!

Nutritional Value:
Calories: 460
Carbs: 45g
Protein: 40g
Fats: 10g

Tasty Teriyaki Salmon and Fried Rice

Ingredients:
1 Salmon fillet
50g White rice
1 Egg
Green vegetables
1 Tsp Coconut oil

Ingredients and Method for the Teriyaki Sauce:
In a small bowl, add and mix together
2 Tablespoons of soy sauce
1 Teaspoon of white wine vinegar
1 Tablespoon of honey
1 Clove of garlic chopped
1cm piece of ginger finely grated
1 Teaspoon of cornflour

Method:
- Season the salmon with salt, pepper and chilli flakes
- Using Cooking spray, pan fry the salmon on each side for 5 minutes until cooked
- Add the pre-boiled rice to a frying pan with coconut oil, seasoned
- Crack one egg into the rice and cook for a further 5 minutes on high heat
- Add the teriyaki sauce to the salmon 1 minute before the salmon is cooked (feel free to save some sauce for pouring over once served)
- Serve with green vegetables
- Enjoy!

Nutritional Value:
Calories: 615
Carbs: 50g
Protein: 42g
Fats: 22g

Teriyaki sauce:
Calories: 100

Cajun Prawn Stir Fry with Soy and Garlic Sauce

Ingredients:
200g Prawns
1 Pack Ramen noodles
Vegetables of choice
1tsp Cajun seasoning
Small bunch of coriander chopped
Pepper
Salt

Ingredients and Method for Soy and Garlic sauce:
Mix in a small bowl
1 Tbsp soy sauce
1 Clove garlic crushed
Salt
Chilli flakes

Method:
- Season prawns with pepper, coriander and Cajun seasoning
- Pan fry with cooking spray your chopped vegetables for 5 minutes seasoning with salt, pepper and fresh chilli
- Add the seasoned prawns to cook for 5 minutes
- Add half the sauce to the pan and leave to cook for a further 2 minutes
- Cook the noodles as per packet instructions, and once cooked, add to the prawns and vegetables
- Add the rest of the sauce and heat for a further 2 minutes
- Serve with a lemon wedge
- Enjoy!

Nutritional Value:
Calories: 312
Carbs: 30g
Protein: 34g
Fats: 9g

Jordan's Moroccan Lamb Cutlets with Quinoa

Ingredients:
2x Lamb cutlets
50g Quinoa
1 Carrot
½ Red onion
1 Tbsp balsamic vinegar
Small bunch of rosemary and thyme chopped
2 Tsp cinnamon
1 Tsp paprika
½ Tin tinned tomatoes
Small bunch of chopped parsley
½ Handful raisins
Vine of tomatoes
Salt
Pepper

Method:
- Season lamb cutlets with rosemary, thyme, salt and pepper
- Slice carrots and red onion
- Preheat oven at 200c and place the lamb on a baking tray with the sliced carrots and red onion, adding balsamic vinegar and cover with tin foil
- Cook the lamb for 30-40 minutes (to desired taste)
- Cook the quinoa as per packet instructions
- Combine 1 teaspoon of paprika, 2 teaspoons of cinnamon, half a tin of chopped tomatoes and chopped parsley and mix into a small pan and heat for 2-3 minutes
- Add the cooked quinoa into the combined mixture and cook for a further 5 minutes, season if needed
- Add the cooked lamb cutlets and raisins and leave to simmer for 5 minutes
- Serve with a vine of tomatoes
- Enjoy!

Nutritional Value:
Calories: 620
Carbs: 44g
Protein: 34g
Fats: 28g

Pesto Pasta with Chicken

Ingredients:
200g Chicken
40g Penne pasta
Handful of spinach
Handful of cherry tomatoes
1 Tbsp red or green pesto
Garlic salt
Pepper
Basil

Method:
- Cook the pasta according to its package directions
- Whilst the pasta is cooking, heat some cooking spray in a large pan over medium-high heat for 2 minutes
- Add the chicken to the pan to cook, adding garlic salt and pepper to season (make sure you turn the chicken over and remove from heat once it is cooked through)
- Once the pasta is cooked and drained, add the pesto to the pasta and stir well
- In a large bowl, add the spinach and tomatoes sliced
- Add the pesto pasta to the large bowl and the cooked chicken sliced on top
- Serve with fresh basil
- Enjoy!

Nutritional Value:
Calories: 420
Carbs: 34g
Protein: 40g
Fats: 7g

Beefy Boy Burrito

Ingredients:
150g Minced beef
2 Small wholemeal wraps
½ Avocado
1 Beef tomato sliced
50g Kidney beans
50g Mixed peppers
1 Tsp Smoked paprika
1 Tsp Chilli powder
1 Garlic cloves crushed
1 Onion
Salt and pepper
1 Lime
Chilli flakes
Mixed salad

Method:
- Heat some cooking spray into a saucepan and gently fry the onion and garlic until cooked but still soft
- Add the minced beef, mixed peppers, and kidney beans and continue to cook and stir until the minced beef is brown
- Add in the herbs, spices, and tomatoes and stir thoroughly
- Allow to simmer for 15 minutes and occasionally stir whilst preparing the guacamole

Method for Guacamole:
- Destone the avocado and scoop half into a bowl
- Add the juice from one lime, then season to taste with garlic salt, pepper, and chilli flakes
- Mix and stir with a fork to combine the ingredients
- Now the guacamole is complete, heat your wraps in the microwave for 10 seconds
- Add the beef mince to your wraps served with salad and your homemade guacamole
- Enjoy!

Nutritional Value:
Calories: 555
Carbs: 44g
Protein: 42g
Fats: 22g

Mild Spice Chicken Curry

Ingredients:
2 x Boneless chicken thighs
50g White basmati rice
1 Onion
2 x Beef tomatoes
2 Tbsp Garam Masala
1 Tbsp mild chilli powder
2 Tsp curry powder
1 Tsp cumin
1 Garlic clove crushed

Method:
- Add cooking spray to your pan and place on medium heat, add in the chopped onion and garam masala and cook for 3 mins
- Then add in the chopped tomatoes with 150ml of hot water and leave to stew for 10 mins
- Add in the chopped chicken thighs with the rest of the spices and leave to cook on low for 30 mins, adding more water if necessary
- Whilst the curry is left to simmer, cook rice as per packet instructions
- Once cooked add to a large bowl and top with the curry
- Enjoy!

Nutritional Value:
Calories: 400
Carbs: 32g
Protein: 38g
Fats: 12g

Simply Soy and Butter Pasta

Ingredients:
50g Spaghetti
100g mixed mushrooms
2tbsp soy sauce
1tbsp butter
Small bunch of chives chopped
Salt and pepper

Method:
- Cook the spaghetti as per packet instructions. Once cooked, drain the pasta but set aside one cup of the cooking water
- Heat the cooking spray into a frying pan and add garlic and mushrooms. Cook until browned
- Add the soy sauce and butter to the frying pan and allow to bubble
- Add the cooked pasta along with a tbsp of the cooking water and mix together
- Add the chives and seasoning before serving
- Serve into a large bowl and Enjoy

Nutritional Value:
Calories: 290
Carbs: 34g
Protein: 9g
Fats: 13g

High Carb

7

Post-Workout Meals

Jordan's Oatmeal with Dark Chocolate

Ingredients:
50g Oats
1 Scoop protein powder
200ml Unsweetened oat milk
2 Squares dark chocolate
60g Blueberries

Method:
- Combine oats and protein powder
- Mix with water or oat milk
- Top with shredded dark chocolate and blueberries
- Enjoy!

Nutritional Value:
Calories: 560
Carbs: 70g
Protein: 30g
Fats: 13g

Salmon, Egg and Cream Cheese on Sourdough Bread

Ingredients:
1 Slice of Sourdough bread
80g Smoked salmon
30g Cream cheese
1 Egg
1 Banana, mixed berries

Method:
- Boil a pan of water. Once the water is boiling, crack the egg into the water to poach for 4 minutes
- Leave the sourdough bread cold or toast it, spread cream cheese finely, and add the salmon on top
- Add the egg once poached
- Serve with salt, pepper, chilli flakes, and lemon wedge
- Enjoy!

Nutritional Value:
Calories: 620
Carbs: 55g
Protein: 32g
Fats: 24g

Healthy Granola

Ingredients:
1 Tbsp olive oil
1 Tbsp maple syrup
1 Tbsp honey
1 Tsp vanilla extract
60g Rolled oats
20g Sunflower seed
1 Tbsp sesame seeds
20g Pumpkin seeds
25g Flaked almond
25g Dried berries (find them in the baking aisle)
15g Coconut flakes

Method:
- Preheat oven to 150c
- Mix the coconut oil, maple syrup, honey, and vanilla into a bowl
- Tip in the remaining ingredients, excluding dried fruit and coconut
- Add the granola onto two baking sheets and spread evenly, and bake for 15 minutes
- Remove the granola from the oven and mix in the dried fruit and coconut and bake for a further 15 minutes
- Once baked, scrape the granola onto a flat tray/plate to cool
- Once cooled, you can serve with unsweetened almond milk
- The granola can also be stored in an airtight container for up to a week in a cool place
- Enjoy!

Nutritional Value:
Calories: 700
Carbs: 95g
Protein: 24g
Fats: 28g

Breakfast Bagel

Ingredients:
1 Bagel
2 x Lean protein

Method:
- Your choice of protein (chicken sausage, bacon, egg) pick two
- Coat a frying pan with cooking spray
- Cook up your chosen protein
- Remove protein from the pan
- Toast your bagel
- Cook the egg to your desired texture
- Serve with a sauce of your choice
- Enjoy!

Nutritional Value:
Calories: 580
Carbs: 50g
Protein: 42g
Fats: 18g

Acai Bowl

Ingredients:
150ml Apple juice
1 Banana
60g Frozen berries
60g Vanilla Greek yogurt
1 Tbsp honey
½ Packet of frozen acai berry puree, broken into pieces

Method:
· Place the apple juice, banana, frozen berries, yogurt, honey, and acai puree into the blender
· Blend until smooth
· Pour into a deep bowl
· Top with your desired toppings
· Enjoy!

Nutritional Value:
Calories: 440
Carbs: 80g
Protein: 7g
Fats: 7g

Chilli and Coriander Prawns with Pasta

Ingredients:
150g prawns
80g pasta (spaghetti)
Cherry tomatoes
Mixed peppers
¼ tin tinned tomatoes
2 Tbsp passata
Red chilli pepper
Small bunch of coriander
Salt

Method:
- Boil a pan of water on high heat, adding a pinch of salt
- Season prawns with the coriander and one red chilli sliced, leave to one side
- Add the pasta to the pan of water and cook to the on-pack instructions
- When the pasta is nearly cooked add the prawns to a frying pan and cook with the tomatoes and peppers for 5 mins
- Once the pasta is cooked, drain out the water and add to the pan with the prawns
- Stir in the tinned tomatoes and passata, leave to simmer for 5 mins
- Serve with fresh parsley
- Enjoy!

Nutritional Value:
Calories: 420
Carbs: 64g
Protein: 35g
Fats: 4g

Champion's Sandwich

Ingredients:
3 Slices wholemeal bread
100g Chicken
1 Avocado
Lettuce
Tomato
1 Tbsp mayonnaise

Method:
- Slice your tomatoes and avocado
- Finely spread mayonnaise onto one side of the 3 slices of the wholemeal bread
- On one slice of bread, add on top of the mayonnaise some lettuce, sliced avocado and tomato
- Now add your pre-cooked and sliced chicken, add seasoning
- Add another slice of bread on top of the chicken, mayonnaise side up
- Repeat the process above
- Add the last slice of bread mayonnaise side down
- Serve sliced in half
- Enjoy !

Nutritional Value:
Calories: 580
Carbs: 56g
Protein: 34g
Fats: 27g

TOP TIP

Add in some chicken for extra protein

Jordan's Mushroom Risotto

Ingredients:
20g Dried porcini mushrooms
150g Chestnut mushrooms, chopped
1 Vegetable stock cube
1 Tbsp olive oil
1 Onion, finely chopped
1 Garlic clove, finely chopped

80g Risotto rice
2 Tbsp apple cider vinegar
1 Tsp butter
Handful parsley leaves, chopped
20g Parmesan, freshly grated

Method:
- Place the porcini mushrooms into a large bowl and pour over 1 litre of boiling water and leave to soak for 20 minutes
- Then drain into another bowl, discarding the last few tbsp of liquid
- Crumble 1 vegetable stock cube into the mushroom liquid, then squeeze the mushrooms to remove any liquid from them
- Add your finely chopped onion and garlic and cook for 3-4 minutes or until soft
- Stir in the chopped chestnut mushrooms and dried mushrooms, season with salt and pepper, and continue to cook for a further 8 minutes until the mushrooms are soft
- Add the risotto rice into the pan and cook for 1 minute, add 2 tbsp of apple cider vinegar and a ¼ of the mushroom stock and continue to cook
- Simmer the rice, stirring often, until the rice has absorbed all the liquid
- Add the same amount of stock again and continue to simmer and stir (it should now start to become creamy and tender)
- Add the final stock amount and continue to stir until the rice is cooked
- If the rice is still undercooked add a splash of water and continue to cook
- Once cooked, remove the pan from the heat, add the butter, parmesan cheese and freshly chopped parsley
- Leave to cool for a few minutes and the rice can then take up any excess liquid whilst cooling
- Stir once more and serve into a large bowl, add the last of the parmesan cheese and parsley leaves
- Enjoy!

Nutritional Value:
Calories: 420
Carbs: 64g
Protein: 12g
Fats: 17g

Dirty Sweet Potato Fries

Ingredients:
300g Sweet potato
Tomatoes
Chilli pepper
Jalapenos
25g Feta
2 Tbsp Cajun seasoning
1 Tbsp light mayonnaise
Chilli flakes
Fresh chopped parsley
Salt
Pepper

Method:
- Peel the outer layer of your sweet potato and slice into fries
- Preheat oven to 200c
- Mix cornflour, salt, pepper, and 2 tsp of Cajun together in a bowl
- Add the sliced sweet potato and mix well to coat
- Add 2 tbsp of olive oil and massage into the sweet potato
- Add the seasoned sweet potato onto a large baking tray with tin foil and cook for 20-25 minutes
- Finely slice a chilli pepper, tomatoes and jalapenos pepper (if not already)
- Once the sweet potato fries are cooked, remove from the oven and add to a plate or bowl
- Leave to cool for 2 minutes and add on top the mayonnaise, tomatoes, chilli pepper and jalapenos
- Crumble on top the feta cheese
- Serve adding chilli flakes and fresh parsley
- Enjoy!

Nutritional Value:
Calories: 400
Carbs: 62g
Protein: 8g
Fats: 14g

Sweet Potato Cottage Pie

Ingredients:
150g Beef mince
300g Sweet potato
1 Onion
100g Carrots
80g Sweet peppers
Peas
25g Cheddar cheese
1 Garlic clove chopped
1 Tbsp butter
¼ Tin tinned tomatoes
2 Tbsp passata
Salt
Pepper
Chopped fresh parsley

Method:
- Bring a saucepan of water to boil, add the chopped sweet potatoes, boil for 15 minutes and then drain
- Mash together with a tbsp of butter then season with salt and pepper
- Heat a deep-frying pan over medium heat and add cooking spray
- Add your finely sliced onions and fry for 2-3 minutes
- Add the garlic, peas, and carrots, cook until soft
- Over medium heat in another frying pan add cooking spray and the mince and cook until browned
- Once cooked, add the mince to the other frying pan and add the tinned tomatoes, passata and bring to a simmer
- Preheat the oven to 190c
- Layer the mince mix in an ovenproof dish and top with the sweet potato mash
- Add to the oven and cook for 20 minutes
- Remove after 20 minutes and add the grated cheese on top and place back in the oven and cook for a further 10 minutes
- Serve in a bowl and season with salt and pepper and fresh parsley
- Enjoy!

Nutritional Value:
Calories: 800
Carbs: 70g
Protein: 43g
Fats: 35g

Chicken Sausage Noodle Stir Fry with Soy and Sweet Chilli Sauce

Ingredients:
3 Chicken sausages
80g Noodles
Mangetout
Sweet peppers
 Mushrooms
Baby corn
Salt
Pepper

Method:
- Cut your chicken sausages into several pieces and slice your stir fry vegetables
- Add cooking spray to a deep frying pan and heat on a medium heat
- Place your chopped chicken sausage pieces into the frying pan and add seasoning
- After 3 minutes, add your stir fry vegetables and cook for a further 5 minutes, cook the noodles as per packet instructions
- Whilst the noodles cook, place your stir fry on a low heat and continue to stir
- Add in your homemade sweet chilli sauce and cook for a further 1 minute
- Once cooked, add your noodles to a deep bowl
- Place your chicken sausage stir fry with chilli sauce on top
- Serve with fresh parsley
- Enjoy!

Method for Sweet Chilli Sauce:
- Simply take some hot sauce and add 1 tbsp of honey

Nutritional Value:
Calories: 500
Carbs: 66g
Protein: 38g
Fats: 12g

Thai Prawn Curry

Ingredients:
150g Prawns
60g White rice
½ Onion
1 Garlic clove crushed
1 Chilli pepper sliced
Handful of tomatoes
1/2 Tin of light coconut milk
2 Tbsp Red Thai Paste

Method:
- Heat 2 tbsp of olive oil in a deep pan over medium heat, add the sliced onion, garlic, and chilli pepper for 2-3 minutes
- Stir in the curry paste and cook for a further 1 minute
- Add the chopped tomatoes and coconut milk and bring to boil
- Leave to simmer for 5 minutes
- If the mixture seems too thick, add a little boiling water
- Add the prawns and cook for 8- 10 minutes
- Cook rice as per packet instructions
- Once cooked, add rice to a deep bowl and add the Thai Prawn Curry on top
- Serve with vegetables of choice and freshly chopped coriander
- Enjoy!

Nutritional Value:
Calories: 515
Carbs: 60g
Protein: 35g
Fats: 18g

Teriyaki Chicken Stir Fry

Ingredients:
150g Chicken
80g Noodles
Mangetout
Baby corn
Sugar snap peas

For the Teriyaki Sauce:
1 Tbsp light soy
1 Tbsp honey
1 Tsp cornflour
1 Tsp rice wine vinegar
1 Garlic clove crushed
1 cm piece ginger finely sliced

Method:
- Slice and season your chicken with salt and pepper
- In a deep-frying pan, add cooking spray on a medium heat, add the sliced chicken and garlic and cook on each side for 3-5 minutes
- Add your sliced and stir fry vegetables and cook for a further 4 minutes, until the vegetables have browned and softened
- Cook your noodles as per packet instructions
- Add your homemade sauce to the chicken stir fry and cook for a further 2 minutes
- Once cooked, add the noodles to a deep bowl
- Place on top your cooked chicken stir fry
- Garnish with a small amount of sesame seeds
- Enjoy!

Nutritional Value:
Calories: 460
Carbs: 62g
Protein: 34g
Fats: 5g

Chicken Tray Bake with White Rice

Ingredients:
1 Chicken leg
40g Chorizo
60g White rice
Mixed peppers
Broccoli
Courgette
Onion
1 Tbsp Garlic oil
1 Tbsp Chili oil
2 Tbsp smoked paprika
1 Chilli pepper finely sliced
Salt
Pepper
1 Tbsp honey

Method:
- Slice your vegetables and chorizo
- Preheat oven to 190c
- Using a large baking tray, add cooking spray and a tbsp of garlic oil
- Add vegetables, chorizo, sliced chilli pepper, salt, and pepper to the baking tray
- Add 2 tbsp of smoked paprika on top of the vegetables
- Marinate chicken with chilli oil, smoked paprika, and Cajun powder
- Add the marinated chicken on top of the vegetables and add to the oven and cook for 40 minutes
- After 40 minutes, remove the baking tray, add honey on top of the chicken and cook for a further 10 minutes, increasing oven heat to 200c
- Cook the rice as per packet instructions
- Remove the baking tray and remove the vegetables and chicken, place on a large bowl/plate
- Add the cooked rice to the baking tray with the liquid and mix together
- Once mixed, the rice should have soaked most of the liquid and it is now ready to add to a deep bowl
- Add the vegetables and chicken on top
- Squeeze a lemon on top of the dish and serve with freshly chopped coriander
- Enjoy!

Nutritional Value:
Calories: 880
Carbs: 65g
Protein: 42g
Fats: 30g

Sticky Beef with Rice

Ingredients:
1 Beef Steak
60g Jasmine rice
1 Onion
Handful of mushrooms
Pak choi
Green beans
½ Chili pepper

For the sauce:
1 Tbsp soy
1 Tbsp maple syrup
1 Tsp rice wine vinegar
1 Tsp cornflour
Finely sliced chili pepper and garlic

Method:
- Slice the beef, onions, chilli pepper and mushrooms
- Marinate the beef in the homemade sauce
- Heat a deep frying pan with cooking spray on a medium heat adding the onions, garlic, and chilli pepper and cook for 3 minutes
- Add the sliced beef and cook on both sides for 2 minutes and add the mushrooms then cook for a further 2 minutes
- Remove from the heat and leave to one side
- Cook the rice as per packet instructions
- Heat the frying pan with the beef and vegetables on a low heat with the rest of the sauce and cook for a further 2 minutes
- Place the cooked rice in a deep bowl and add the sticky beef on top
- Serve with freshly chopped parsley
- Enjoy!

Nutritional Value:
Calories: 650
Carbs: 70g
Protein: 48g
Fats: 16g

Sweet Jacket Potato with Tuna Mayo

Ingredients:
1 Large sweet potato
1 Tin of tuna in spring water
Sweetcorn
Red onion
Salt
Pepper
Light mayo

Method:
- Preheat oven to 180c
- Rinse the sweet potato and pat dry and pierce in several places
- Place on a microwavable plate/dish and microwave on each side for 4 minutes or until soft
- Once soft, add the sweet potato onto a baking tray with tin foil and cook in the oven for a further 4- 5 minutes or until the potato skin is browned
- In a bowl, mix the drained tuna and sweetcorn, salt, pepper, red onion, and mayonnaise
- Once the sweet potato is cooked add to a plate and slice down the middle
- Add your tuna mayo mixture
- Serve with chilli flakes or pepper
- Enjoy!

Nutritional Value:
Calories: 400
Carbs: 62g
Protein: 26g
Fats: 2g

Spiced Lamb with Couscous

Ingredients:
1 Lamb shank
60g Couscous
Cherry tomatoes
Courgette
Mixed peppers
Red onion
1 Tbsp olive oil
1 Garlic clove crushed
2 Sprigs of thyme
Salt
Pepper

For the sauce:
Use a mini chopper or shake together in a bottle
2 Red chillies finely sliced
2 Garlic cloves crushed
½ Tsp salt
½ Tsp cayenne pepper
½ Tsp paprika
½ Lemon squeezed
1 Cup of water

Method:
- Preheat the oven to 180c
- Season the lamb with olive oil, salt, pepper, thyme, and garlic
- Place on a baking tray with tin foil and add to the oven and cook for 40 minutes
- Slice your vegetables and add to a baking tray with tin foil
- Spray with cooking spray and add salt, pepper, and smoked paprika
- After 10 minutes of cooking the lamb, add the vegetables to the oven and cook for 30 minutes
- Once nearly cooked, follow the on-pack instructions for the couscous
- Serve the lamb on top of the couscous with the vegetables and hot sauce
- Enjoy!

Nutritional Value:
Calories: 720
Carbs: 55g
Protein: 60g
Fats: 24g

Steak Fajitas

Ingredients:
200g Steak
2 Tortilla wraps
1 Onion
Mixed peppers
Jalapenos
Spices
Salt
Pepper

Method:
- Slice the steak into thin strips and season with salt and pepper
- Slice all the vegetables into thin strips
- In a large frying pan, add 2 tbsp of olive oil and turn the heat to high
- Add all the vegetables and cook for 7-10 minutes or until charred
- Remove the vegetables from the heat and store in the oven at 100c to stay warm
- Add the steak to the hot frying pan and fry for 6-8 minutes, longer for more well done
- Season with salt and pepper or the spices of your choosing
- Using tortilla wraps, wrap the vegetables and steak to serve
- Add sour cream or crema if desired
- Enjoy!

Nutritional Value:
Calories: 460
Carbs: 54g
Protein: 40g
Fats: 15g

Easy Chicken Fried Rice

Ingredients:
200g Chicken
70g Brown rice
Pak choi
Tenderstem broccoli
½ Onion
1 Tbsp olive oil
1 Red chili
1 Egg
1 Tsp Chinese five spice
Spring onion
Salt
Pepper

Method:
- Preheat oven to 190c
- Slice the onion, spring onion, and chilli pepper finely
- Season the chicken breast with Chinese five-spice, salt, and pepper and mix in with a tbsp of olive oil
- Add the seasoned chicken to a baking tray with tin foil, add a lemon slice and cook in the oven for 30 minutes
- Cook the rice as per packet instructions
- Heat a frying pan with cooking spray on medium-low heat
- Add onion, garlic, chilli pepper and cook for 2 minutes and then add the rice and mix together
- Crack one egg into the frying pan and mix together with the rice and vegetables for 2 minutes
- Once cooked add the fried rice to a deep bowl and place the chicken sliced on top
- Serve with a garnish of spring onion
- Enjoy!

Nutritional Value:
Calories: 480
Carbs: 64g
Protein: 52g
Fats: 18g

Fresh Penne Pasta with Spinach, Pea, and Poached Egg

Ingredients:
1 Egg
80g Penne pasta
1 Courgette
30g Frozen peas
2 Handfuls spinach
250ml vegetable stock
Small bunch mint leaves and parsley
1 Tbsp olive oil
2 Tbsp white wine vinegar
½ Lemon
1 Garlic clove finely chopped
100ml Unsweetened almond milk
Sprinkle of Parmesan Cheese
Salt
Pepper

Method:
- Heat the oil in a pan, add the courgette, season with salt and cook for 10 minutes or until soft
- Add the zest of lemon, garlic, and white wine vinegar to the pan and cook for a further 5 mins on low
- Tip in the stock and milk, stir, then add the pasta and leave to simmer for 15 mins
- Add the spinach and stir, leave for a further 2 mins
- Add the finely chopped mint leaves and season with salt and pepper
- Serve up in a deep bowl with a sprinkle of parmesan cheese
- Enjoy!

Nutritional Value:
Calories: 450
Carbs: 66g
Protein: 11g
Fats: 18g

8

Snacks
and Treats

Take a look at my snacks and treats section. You will notice you have two snacks on both the training day plan and non-training day plan. Feel free to add an extra snack throughout the day if you are feeling lethargic, low on energy, or need a few extra calories for an event that day.

Be mindful that they still contain calories, so if the overall goal is to change your body composition, then stick to the plan.

Rice Cakes with Banana and Peanut Putter

Ingredients:

2 Rice cakes
1 Banana
1 Tbsp Peanut butter

Method:

Spread the rice cake with peanut butter and add sliced banana on top.

Ryvita with Cottage Cheese and Chilli Flakes

Ingredients:

2 Ryvita
150g Cottage cheese
Chilli flakes

Method:

Spread the Ryvita with cottage cheese and add chilli flakes.

Hummus with carrot sticks

Ingredients:

100g Hummus
Carrot sticks

Method:

Serve up the hummus with carrot sticks.

Apple slices and peanut butter

Ingredients:

1 Apple
1 Tbsp peanut butter

Method:

Slice up the apple, and dip in the peanut butter.

Low-calorie popcorn with dark chocolate and pistachio nuts

Ingredients:

40g Low-calorie popcorn
2 Squares dark chocolate 75%
30g Pistachio nuts

Method:

Perfect treat for a Friday night in with Netflix.

Melt the dark chocolate and pour over the popcorn, finish with chopped pistachio nuts.

Fruit bowl

Ingredients:

1 apple, ½ orange, 60g mixed berries, add to a bowl, and squirt over fresh lemon.

Green Monster Smoothie

Ingredients:

½ Cucumber
½ Handful Spinach
½ Handful kale
½ Avocado
2 Sprigs fresh mint
1 Kiwifruit
1 cup Water
½ of Apple
Squirt of lemon

Method:

Blend all together and enjoy.

Cocoa smoothie: Get the dopamine flowing with raw cocoa

Ingredients:

1 Tbsp dark cocoa powder
½ Cup coconut milk
½ Cup strawberries
1 Cup of ice

Method:

Blend all together and enjoy.

Banana Ice Cream

Ingredients:

1 Banana
250ml Unsweetened almond milk
1 Scoop vanilla protein
Cashew nuts
Fresh fruit of choice

Method:

- Chop the banana into chunks
- Lay on a tray with greaseproof paper and place in the freezer overnight
- Tip the frozen banana into a blender with almond milk, vanilla protein powder and blend until smooth
- Serve topped with cashew nuts or fruit.

Chocolate Custard Pots

TOP TIP

I like to add fresh raspberries and mint to mine

Ingredients:

150ml Low fat custard
30g Dark chocolate (broken into pieces)
Grated zest of ½ orange
Sprinkle of cardamom

Method:

- Gently heat the custard in a pan
- Add the chocolate, zest, and cardamon
- Stir until the chocolate has melted and sieve into a jug
- Pour into a small pot and fridge for at least 4hours to firm up
- Remove from the fridge and serve.

Homemade granola with greek yogurt

Ingredients:

1 Tbsp olive oil
1 Tbsp maple syrup
1 Tbsp honey
1 Tsp vanilla extract
50g Rolled oats
2 Tsp sunflower seed
1 Tbsp sesame seeds
1 Tbsp pumpkin seeds
30g Flaked almond
40g Dried berries
20g Coconut flakes or
desiccated coconut

Method:

STEP 1
Heat oven to 150C/fan 130C/
gas 2. Mix the oil, maple
syrup, honey, and vanilla
in a large bowl. Tip in all
the remaining ingredients,
except the dried fruit and
coconut, and mix well.

STEP 2
Tip the granola onto a
baking sheet and spread
evenly. Bake for 15 mins,
then mix in the coconut
and dried fruit, and bake
for 10-15 mins more.
Remove and scrape onto a
flat tray to cool. Serve with
Greek yogurt.

Low cal rice pudding

Ingredients:

100g Pudding rice
400ml Unsweetened
almond milk
1tbsp Honey

Method:

- In a saucepan, place
  the rice, milk, honey,
  and 100ml of water.
  Boil for 20 mins
- Stir until the texture
  becomes thick and
  creamy
- Remove from heat and
  serve in a bowl.

Tip:

This gives you a blank
canvas, so get creative.
I like to add in fresh fruit
and peanut butter.
Or it's perfect after a
tough gym session. Add in
a scoop of vanilla protein.

Spiced Nut Mix

Ingredients:

100g Cashews and
almonds mixed
1 Tbsp Olive oil
1 Tsp Cumin
1 Tsp Paprika

Method:

- Add all the ingredients
  onto an oven tray
- Cook on 180c for 15
  mins
- Remove from the oven
  and season with salt.

Tip:

These can store in an
airtight container for up
to 5 days. Why not make
a batch, so you always
have a snack ready for you
when on the road.

9
Take the
HIT

HIIT training

HIIT or high-intensity interval training is the style of training we will be using in my book. But what is it? HIIT is a method of exercise that requires you to alternate between periods of slow, steady, and gradual exercise for a set amount of time and fast-paced, high-intensity exercise for another set amount of time.

A very simple example of HIIT would be to walk for 30 seconds, sprint for 30 seconds, and repeat the entire process for several rounds. You will vary your speed and the intensity in which you perform the exercise for the entire duration of your workout. My HIIT sessions last 20 to 35 minutes on average, and whilst that may not sound like much, as you are pushing your body so much, you can potentially burn off even more calories than you would during a 60 – 90-minute gym session performed at a moderate pace.

The beauty behind HIIT training
Is the amount of calories you burn afterwards when you are in recovery.

This process is called EPOC (excess post-exercise oxygen consumption). It refers to the increased oxygen level your body consumes and calories it burns to recover from working out. So, the harder you train in your HIIT session, the more calories your body will need and can still be burning for up to 18 hours after the session is complete. That is also why getting in three HIIT sessions per week would be ideal.

HIIT for everyone
Everyone can take part in some HIIT training, choose what your current fitness levels are or any injuries you may have. They are easily adaptable, and you can pretty much turn any exercise into HIIT style. For example, go from a slow walk into a power walk, or a slow swim into a fast-paced swim and cycle through the process.

My workouts are also designed to be done in your own home, no need for a gym membership. But for those of you who attend a gym feel free to take the workouts with you.

The workout breakdown
The workouts will be broken down into two different categories:

Bodyweight HIIT
Resistance HIIT

This is so your body can feel the benefits from both and stop you getting bored. Always making it exciting. Please check out my social media pages for extra workouts. You can choose any workout in any order you like; there are no rules.

Workout to feel great

Studies show that the brain releases more serotonin (the feel-good hormone) after a workout.

So, take note once you have completed a tough workout, you will feel great afterwards; that's the same reason I like to train in the morning or go for a walk. It sets me up for the day's challenges.

You will have read earlier in the book the close connection between the food you eat and your mood. You are now covering both areas with this book - nutrition and exercise. It is because of this you will be on the road to living a healthier and happier fulfilled life.

Dopamine

The motivation hormone: WHY am I mentioning this? Well, most people think dopamine is a feel-good hormone, when in fact, it's not. It's the motivation hormone. Which we can all agree is very important when following a plan or even completing any life task. If you had zero motivation, you would not succeed and just get stale and plod along.

So, here's something I want to introduce, THE DOPAMINE REWARDS BANK. I will show you how to use this effectively and use the motivation you create. The brain releases dopamine at a low rate, so we need to make the most of it and make it a recurring experience. But how?

Think back to a time when you have completed a task or a goal. It could be anything from passing your driving test, getting the promotion, being the best player on the field, or completing a task your employer gave you. Well, that feeling you get, the high, is the dopamine kicking in. You should then notice when you are on that high, and you want to carry on doing more things to keep the roll going. But then, soon enough, that time will pass, and it may not return for weeks, months, or some people years.

So, what we need to create is a rewards scheme that encourages you to achieve that feeling more often. Celebrate the process then motivation will be at a high, making you want to carry on. It will make it almost addictive to succeed.

For example, follow the plan 100% for five days straight, then reward yourself with a meal out with family or friends, make sure you celebrate and relish in that positively high feeling.

Hold on to that motivation, then get back on the plan. You will then create a pattern, and your brain will become more productive at releasing dopamine.

Now I'm not saying you have to reward yourself with food or a drink, etc., but make sure you do celebrate those little tasks. When I record a new cooking video or create new content for you, I take myself into a quiet room, play some feel-good music blasting into my ears and celebrate the amazing things I've just created. It then drives me on to do more.

Section 1 Bodyweight HIIT:

Workout 1-

30 seconds on each exercise with 20 second rest.
Complete x 10 rounds in total (take a breather after each round).

1.   Squats

2.   Alt Lunges

3.   Jumping squats

4. Press ups

5. Mountain climbers

Workout 2-

40 seconds on 20 seconds off each exercise.
Complete x 10 rounds in as little rest as possible.

1.   Crunches

2.   Leg raises

3.   High knees

4. Burpees

5. Mountain climbers

Section 2: Resistance HIIT

Equipment needed-
- x 2 Dumbbells 2kg or 4kg
- x 1 Kettlebell 6kg or 10kg

Workout 1-

40 seconds on, 20 seconds rest.
Complete this circuit x 10 with 1 min rest between each circuit.

1.   KB squat

2.   KB alternating reverse lunges

3.   KB sumo squats

4.   KB stiff leg deadlifts

5.   KB hip thrust

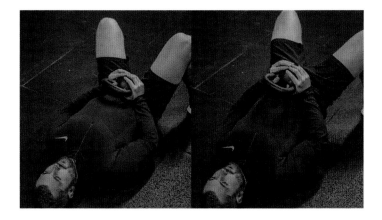

Workout 2-

30 seconds on, 10 second rest.
Complete this circuit x 10 with 30 seconds to 1 min rest between each circuit.

1.   DB bicep curl shoulder press

2.   DB lateral raises

3.   DB front raises

4.   KB Jumping squats

5.   KB swings

Workout tips:

Feel free to descale any of the
exercises if they are too difficult or
in case of injury, for example change
from a press up to a press up on your
knees or a jumping squat to a normal
squat.

You can also change the active and
rest times too if you need to make
them harder, less rest, and easier -
rest more.

Plan Your Week

10

My week

	Monday	Tuesday	Wednesday
Morning walk	1 hour walk Before Breakfast	1 hour walk Before Breakfast	1 hour walk Before Breakfast
Meal 1	Banana Porridge Bowl	Fancy French toast with bacon	Cheesy Scrambled eggs with Chorizo
Snack	Rice cakes Banana and Peanut butter	Hummus with carrot sticks	Rice cakes Banana and Peanut butter
Meal 2	Steak and mozzarella salad	Chicken, Chorizo, and feta with spinach	Chicken, Chorizo, and feta with spinach
Snack	Ryvita with cottage cheese	Ryvita with cottage cheese	Apple slices with peanut butter
Workout	HIIT Session	1 hour weights session full body	REST
PWO shake	2 scoops protein powder and 2 squares dark chocolate	2 scoops protein powder and rice pudding	N/A
PWO high carb meal or reduced carb meal	Mushroom risotto	Chicken sausage noodle stir-fry	Cajun prawn stir fry with soy and garlic

Here is an example of how my week usually plans out. I thought this would be useful so you can see what happens over the course of my week—how and what time I train, and what meals I choose from the plan.

You will notice I go for a walk every morning. For me, it is a great way to clear my mind and think of new ideas and get real creative. I put on my headphones and blackout the world. Before my walk, I always have two cups of water and a small black coffee.

I tend to complete my training session later in the afternoon to have my high-carb meal post-workout and later in the day. This suits me and relaxes me at night,

Thursday	Friday	Saturday	Sunday
1 hour walk Before Breakfast	Rest	1 hour walk Before Breakfast	Rest
Banana Porridge Bowl	Feel-good shake	Buckwheat and blueberry jam pancakes	Chocolate orange yogurt bowl
Fruit bowl	Apple slices with peanut butter	Apple slices with peanut butter	Homemade granola with Greek yogurt
Watermelon salad with added Chicken	Steak and asparagus with poached egg	Sticky pork	Almond crusted Cod with Courgetti
Cocoa smoothie	Rice cakes Banana and Peanut butter	Banana ice cream	N/A
HIIT Session	REST	1 hour weights session full body	REST
2 scoops protein powder and 2 squares dark chocolate	N/A	2 scoops protein powder and 2 squares dark chocolate	N/A
Chicken tray- bake with white rice	Moroccan Lamb	Thai prawn curry	Off Plan Meal Usually means going out with friends/family to a restaurant

ready for a good night's sleep. A protein shake after training is excellent for replenishing the muscles and start the recovery process. I add in a piece of dark chocolate for the insulin spike (it gets protein to my muscles faster) but also for the positive dopamine effect.

On a Sunday, I like to rest and have a meal off plan that evening and reflect on the week passed. I sometimes may have another meal off that week too, depending on what I have on - any special occasions, business, family time, etc.

The NU You

Rob Hammond

Jordan is an excellent personal trainer, but his expertise goes way beyond that. Not only is his knowledge on point for training and nutrition he is constantly evolving his methods. He is motivating and personable, helping you every step of the way, both in and out of the gym. When I first met Jordan, I was overweight and knew I needed to lose some serious weight.

We embarked on a tough journey, and I learnt vital training and nutrition knowledge that has set me up for life. He doesn't keep it a secret but teaches you his ways. Now I can manage my own gym routine and diet, keeping me in good lean shape all year round. I owe him a lot and can genuinely say he changed my life. Thanks so much, Jordan!

Jack Crilly

I think Jordan really knows how to engage with his clients, and honestly, I don't think I could look the way I do without him. I first came to Jordan in 2017, asking him the best way to get "shredded" as I wanted to be in good shape for a holiday. Ever since that shred, I've never used anyone else.

Everyone who starts their fitness journey is going to be a bit sceptical whether it's going to work or not? Well, Jordan's motivation alone will be enough to push you into reaching that goal.

Everything you need to know, he will explain. Jordan is very knowledgeable, especially in nutrition, so getting in shape should be no problem.

Not only is he now a good friend but also an amazing personal trainer.

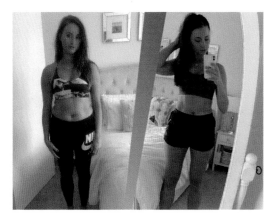

Nicola Thorpe

Jordan was the first personal trainer I've ever felt comfortable with 1:1 training. He's knowledgeable in nutrition, tailoring the program around your dietary needs and lifestyle, making the program easy to maintain and stick to. He is extremely motivating, which as a single parent, I needed that motivation! He pushes you to achieve your best. After training with Jordan, I was in the best physical shape of my life, and I can't wait to get back to it again. I am excited to see what's to come! Honestly can't recommend him enough, and I think my results speak for themselves.

Rachael Scott

I am incredibly uncomfortable at a gym; I always feel out of place, so I needed a personal trainer that made me feel at ease, and Jordan instantly did that. He pushed me to achieve my goals and encouraged me all the way. I've always found his diet plans easy to follow and adapted to suit me. He's always been happy to answer my questions on diet or training, and it's clear he takes pride in what he does. I would recommend Jordan all day long!

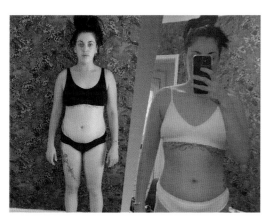

Tara Clegg

Jordan came into my life when I was 1.5 years postpartum. During a time that I was hugely struggling with my weight, which impacted my mental health and confidence. With the introduction of his meals and education, he helped me overcome the obstacles in my way.

The weight started to drop off, and I began to feel much more like myself again. I mean, you can see from my pictures how much weight I have actually lost. The most incredible thing about Jordan is just how approachable he is, and nothing is ever too much hassle, not to mention the gorgeous meal ideas he gives you - like is it even a diet? Jordan has changed my life for the positive and I know I can always rely on him for support and guidance. You're the BEST!

HOW TO CONNECT

Social media platforms:
Instagram: @thetransformationdoctor/ @nubyjs
Facebook: NU by Jordan Storey

Email: jordan@nu-by-js.com
Website: www.nu-by-js.com

The NU App.

The App for NU by Jordan Storey, launched 2022, offers many amazing features, tracks calories, food database, meal logger, goal setting, plan social events so you can enjoy time with friends and still stay on track, built in media platform so you can interact with other NU clients, plus so much more. Make sure you download it today.

ACKNOWLEDGEMENTS

Mum and Dad without them the book would of never happened
Gail Powell for her expertise and patience
Rob Brennan my life coach who opened many doors
All my clients/friends who have supported me over the years, this content is for you.

CREDITS

Food Photography	Jordan Baird/ Baird Visuals
Food Stylist	Nadine McNulty
Branding Design	Lucielle
Cover design and layout	Patrick Ooi
Creative Editor	Gail Powell

INDEX OF RECIPES